First published in the United States in 1991 by
Gallery Books, an imprint of W.H. Smith Publishers, Inc.,
112 Madison Avenue, New York, New York 10016
Copyright © 1986 by The Five Mile Press.
Illustrated by Bob Graham.
Produced by Joshua Morris Publishing, Inc.
in association with The Five Mile Press.
All rights reserved.
Printed in Singapore.
ISBN 0-8317-0931-6

Gallery Books are available for bulk purchase
for sales promotions and premium use. For
details write or telephone the Manager of
Special Sales, W.H. Smith Publishers, Inc.,
112 Madison Avenue, New York, New York 10016,
212/532-6600

Look Out For Rosy!

An early learner book about the senses

bob graham

GALLERY BOOKS
An Imprint of W. H. Smith Publishers Inc.
112 Madison Avenue
New York City 10016

Rosy *hears* the front gate go click.
She uses her *ears*.

She *hears* a *sound*.
It is Mike coming home.

Rosy *sees* Mike.
She uses her *eyes*.

She uses her *sight*.
Watch out Mike!

Rosy flies through the air.
She *feels* the wind on her fur.

The ice cream is cold.
Mike *feels* it on his *skin*.

Down goes Mike!

The ice cream flies
high in the air.

Mike's elbow is sore.
His *skin* hurts.

Rosy is not hurt at all.

But what is this? Rosy is
smelling Mike's ice cream.

She *smells* it with her *nose*.

Too late Mike! Rosy
tastes the ice cream.

She *tastes* it with her *tongue.*
She likes it too!

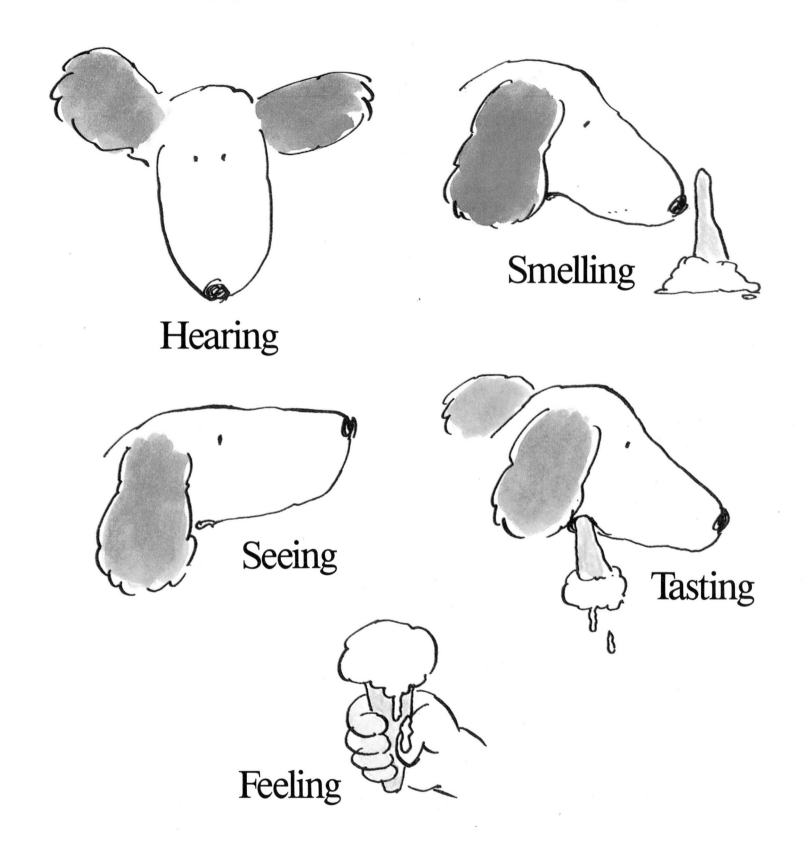

Hearing

Smelling

Seeing

Tasting

Feeling

senses

Senses are the means by which we receive information about what is happening in our environment. External senses provide information about things both far from the body and in contact with it. The senses of hearing and sight are called *distance receiving senses* and respond to very small stimuli. The senses of taste, touch, and smell tell us about things that come in contact with the body.

Experiments to try

1. Ask a child to distinguish between the taste of an apple and a potato. Try this with eyes closed and then with nose blocked. Is it more difficult to distinguish in each of these cases?
2. Whisper something very softly to a child. Can your voice be heard? Try saying the same thing a little louder until the child can repeat what you say.
3. Line up a variety of objects—some with smooth surfaces, some rough, some cold or hot, etc. Ask a child to comment on the difference in feel of each object.
4. Fill plastic containers of the same size with three different items, such as rice, marbles, and raisins. One child shakes each container in turn while the other tries to guess by sound what substance is in which container.